Welcome

Please leave your comments and recommendations in our guest book

Thank you

Places to visit:

Hidden gems:

Recommendations for places to eat or drink:

Places to visit:

Hidden gems:

Recommendations for places to eat or drink:

Places to visit:

Hidden gems:

Recommendations for places to eat or drink:

Places to visit:

Hidden gems:

Recommendations for places to eat or drink:

Places to visit:

Hidden gems:

Recommendations for places to eat or drink:

Places to visit:

Hidden gems:

Recommendations for places to eat or drink:

Places to visit:

Hidden gems:

Recommendations for places to eat or drink:

Places to visit:

Hidden gems:

Recommendations for places to eat or drink:

Places to visit:

Hidden gems:

Recommendations for places to eat or drink:

Places to visit:

Hidden gems:

Recommendations for places to eat or drink:

Places to visit:

Hidden gems:

Recommendations for places to eat or drink:

Places to visit:

Hidden gems:

Recommendations for places to eat or drink:

Places to visit:

Hidden gems:

Recommendations for places to eat or drink:

Places to visit:

Hidden gems:

Recommendations for places to eat or drink:

Places to visit:

Hidden gems:

Recommendations for places to eat or drink:

Places to visit:

Hidden gems:

Recommendations for places to eat or drink:

Places to visit:

Hidden gems:

Recommendations for places to eat or drink:

Places to visit:

Hidden gems:

Recommendations for places to eat or drink:

Places to visit:

Hidden gems:

Recommendations for places to eat or drink:

Places to visit:

Hidden gems:

Recommendations for places to eat or drink:

Places to visit:

Hidden gems:

Recommendations for places to eat or drink:

Places to visit:

Hidden gems:

Recommendations for places to eat or drink:

Places to visit:

Hidden gems:

Recommendations for places to eat or drink:

Places to visit:

Hidden gems:

Recommendations for places to eat or drink:

Places to visit:

Hidden gems:

Recommendations for places to eat or drink:

Places to visit:

Hidden gems:

Recommendations for places to eat or drink:

Places to visit:

Hidden gems:

Recommendations for places to eat or drink:

Places to visit:

Hidden gems:

Recommendations for places to eat or drink:

Places to visit:

Hidden gems:

Recommendations for places to eat or drink:

Places to visit:

Hidden gems:

Recommendations for places to eat or drink:

Places to visit:

Hidden gems:

Recommendations for places to eat or drink:

Places to visit:

Hidden gems:

Recommendations for places to eat or drink:

Places to visit:

Hidden gems:

Recommendations for places to eat or drink:

Places to visit:

Hidden gems:

Recommendations for places to eat or drink:

Places to visit:

Hidden gems:

Recommendations for places to eat or drink:

Places to visit:

Hidden gems:

Recommendations for places to eat or drink:

Places to visit:

Hidden gems:

Recommendations for places to eat or drink:

Places to visit:

Hidden gems:

Recommendations for places to eat or drink:

Places to visit:

Hidden gems:

Recommendations for places to eat or drink:

Places to visit:

Hidden gems:

Recommendations for places to eat or drink:

Places to visit:

Hidden gems:

Recommendations for places to eat or drink:

Places to visit:

Hidden gems:

Recommendations for places to eat or drink:

Places to visit:

Hidden gems:

Recommendations for places to eat or drink:

Places to visit:

Hidden gems:

Recommendations for places to eat or drink:

Places to visit:

Hidden gems:

Recommendations for places to eat or drink:

Places to visit:

Hidden gems:

Recommendations for places to eat or drink:

Places to visit:

Hidden gems:

Recommendations for places to eat or drink:

Places to visit:

Hidden gems:

Recommendations for places to eat or drink:

Places to visit:

Hidden gems:

Recommendations for places to eat or drink:

Places to visit:

Hidden gems:

Recommendations for places to eat or drink:

Places to visit:

Hidden gems:

Recommendations for places to eat or drink:

Places to visit:

Hidden gems:

Recommendations for places to eat or drink:

Places to visit:

Hidden gems:

Recommendations for places to eat or drink:

Places to visit:

Hidden gems:

Recommendations for places to eat or drink:

Places to visit:

Hidden gems:

Recommendations for places to eat or drink:

Places to visit:

Hidden gems:

Recommendations for places to eat or drink:

Places to visit:

Hidden gems:

Recommendations for places to eat or drink:

Places to visit:

Hidden gems:

Recommendations for places to eat or drink:

Places to visit:

Hidden gems:

Recommendations for places to eat or drink:

Places to visit:

Hidden gems:

Recommendations for places to eat or drink:

Places to visit:

Hidden gems:

Recommendations for places to eat or drink:

Places to visit:

Hidden gems:

Recommendations for places to eat or drink:

Places to visit:

Hidden gems:

Recommendations for places to eat or drink:

Places to visit:

Hidden gems:

Recommendations for places to eat or drink:

Places to visit:

Hidden gems:

Recommendations for places to eat or drink:

Places to visit:

Hidden gems:

Recommendations for places to eat or drink:

Places to visit:

Hidden gems:

Recommendations for places to eat or drink:

Places to visit:

Hidden gems:

Recommendations for places to eat or drink:

Places to visit:

Hidden gems:

Recommendations for places to eat or drink:

Places to visit:

Hidden gems:

Recommendations for places to eat or drink:

Places to visit:

Hidden gems:

Recommendations for places to eat or drink:

Places to visit:

Hidden gems:

Recommendations for places to eat or drink:

Places to visit:

Hidden gems:

Recommendations for places to eat or drink:

Places to visit:

Hidden gems:

Recommendations for places to eat or drink:

Places to visit:

Hidden gems:

Recommendations for places to eat or drink:

Places to visit:

Hidden gems:

Recommendations for places to eat or drink:

Places to visit:

Hidden gems:

Recommendations for places to eat or drink:

Places to visit:

Hidden gems:

Recommendations for places to eat or drink:

Places to visit:

Hidden gems:

Recommendations for places to eat or drink:

Places to visit:

Hidden gems:

Recommendations for places to eat or drink:

Places to visit:

Hidden gems:

Recommendations for places to eat or drink:

Places to visit:

Hidden gems:

Recommendations for places to eat or drink:

Places to visit:

Hidden gems:

Recommendations for places to eat or drink:

Places to visit:

Hidden gems:

Recommendations for places to eat or drink:

Places to visit:

Hidden gems:

Recommendations for places to eat or drink:

Places to visit:

Hidden gems:

Recommendations for places to eat or drink:

Places to visit:

Hidden gems:

Recommendations for places to eat or drink:

Places to visit:

Hidden gems:

Recommendations for places to eat or drink:

Places to visit:

Hidden gems:

Recommendations for places to eat or drink:

Places to visit:

Hidden gems:

Recommendations for places to eat or drink:

Places to visit:

Hidden gems:

Recommendations for places to eat or drink:

Places to visit:

Hidden gems:

Recommendations for places to eat or drink:

Places to visit:

Hidden gems:

Recommendations for places to eat or drink:

Places to visit:

Hidden gems:

Recommendations for places to eat or drink:

Places to visit:

Hidden gems:

Recommendations for places to eat or drink:

Places to visit:

Hidden gems:

Recommendations for places to eat or drink:

Places to visit:

Hidden gems:

Recommendations for places to eat or drink:

Places to visit:

Hidden gems:

Recommendations for places to eat or drink:

Places to visit:

Hidden gems:

Recommendations for places to eat or drink:

Places to visit:

Hidden gems:

Recommendations for places to eat or drink:

Places to visit:

Hidden gems:

Recommendations for places to eat or drink:

Places to visit:

Hidden gems:

Recommendations for places to eat or drink:

Places to visit:

Hidden gems:

Recommendations for places to eat or drink:

Places to visit:

Hidden gems:

Recommendations for places to eat or drink:

Places to visit:

Hidden gems:

Recommendations for places to eat or drink:

Places to visit:

Hidden gems:

Recommendations for places to eat or drink:

Places to visit:

Hidden gems:

Recommendations for places to eat or drink:

Places to visit:

Hidden gems:

Recommendations for places to eat or drink:

Places to visit:

Hidden gems:

Recommendations for places to eat or drink:

Places to visit:

Hidden gems:

Recommendations for places to eat or drink:

Places to visit:

Hidden gems:

Recommendations for places to eat or drink:

Places to visit:

Hidden gems:

Recommendations for places to eat or drink:

Places to visit:

Hidden gems:

Recommendations for places to eat or drink:

Places to visit:

Hidden gems:

Recommendations for places to eat or drink:

Places to visit:

Hidden gems:

Recommendations for places to eat or drink:

Places to visit:

Hidden gems:

Recommendations for places to eat or drink:

Places to visit:

Hidden gems:

Recommendations for places to eat or drink:

Places to visit:

Hidden gems:

Recommendations for places to eat or drink:

Places to visit:

Hidden gems:

Recommendations for places to eat or drink:

Places to visit:

Hidden gems:

Recommendations for places to eat or drink:

Places to visit:

Hidden gems:

Recommendations for places to eat or drink:

Places to visit:

Hidden gems:

Recommendations for places to eat or drink:

Places to visit:

Hidden gems:

Recommendations for places to eat or drink:

Places to visit:

Hidden gems:

Recommendations for places to eat or drink:

Places to visit:

Hidden gems:

Recommendations for places to eat or drink:

Places to visit:

Hidden gems:

Recommendations for places to eat or drink:

Places to visit:

Hidden gems:

Recommendations for places to eat or drink:

Places to visit:

Hidden gems:

Recommendations for places to eat or drink:

Places to visit:

Hidden gems:

Recommendations for places to eat or drink:

Places to visit:

Hidden gems:

Recommendations for places to eat or drink:

Places to visit:

Hidden gems:

Recommendations for places to eat or drink:

Places to visit:

Hidden gems:

Recommendations for places to eat or drink:

Places to visit:

Hidden gems:

Recommendations for places to eat or drink:

Places to visit:

Hidden gems:

Recommendations for places to eat or drink:

Places to visit:

Hidden gems:

Recommendations for places to eat or drink:

Places to visit:

Hidden gems:

Recommendations for places to eat or drink:

Places to visit:

Hidden gems:

Recommendations for places to eat or drink:

Places to visit:

Hidden gems:

Recommendations for places to eat or drink:

Places to visit:

Hidden gems:

Recommendations for places to eat or drink:

Places to visit:

Hidden gems:

Recommendations for places to eat or drink:

Places to visit:

Hidden gems:

Recommendations for places to eat or drink:

Places to visit:

Hidden gems:

Recommendations for places to eat or drink:

Places to visit:

Hidden gems:

Recommendations for places to eat or drink:

Places to visit:

Hidden gems:

Recommendations for places to eat or drink:

Places to visit:

Hidden gems:

Recommendations for places to eat or drink:

Places to visit:

Hidden gems:

Recommendations for places to eat or drink:

Places to visit:

Hidden gems:

Recommendations for places to eat or drink:

Places to visit:

Hidden gems:

Recommendations for places to eat or drink:

Places to visit:

Hidden gems:

Recommendations for places to eat or drink:

Places to visit:

Hidden gems:

Recommendations for places to eat or drink:

Places to visit:

Hidden gems:

Recommendations for places to eat or drink:

Places to visit:

Hidden gems:

Recommendations for places to eat or drink:

Places to visit:

Hidden gems:

Recommendations for places to eat or drink:

Places to visit:

Hidden gems:

Recommendations for places to eat or drink:

Places to visit:

Hidden gems:

Recommendations for places to eat or drink:

Places to visit:

Hidden gems:

Recommendations for places to eat or drink:

Places to visit:

Hidden gems:

Recommendations for places to eat or drink:

Places to visit:

Hidden gems:

Recommendations for places to eat or drink:

Places to visit:

Hidden gems:

Recommendations for places to eat or drink:

Places to visit:

Hidden gems:

Recommendations for places to eat or drink:

Places to visit:

Hidden gems:

Recommendations for places to eat or drink:

Places to visit:

Hidden gems:

Recommendations for places to eat or drink:

Places to visit:

Hidden gems:

Recommendations for places to eat or drink:

Places to visit:

Hidden gems:

Recommendations for places to eat or drink:

Places to visit:

Hidden gems:

Recommendations for places to eat or drink:

Places to visit:

Hidden gems:

Recommendations for places to eat or drink:

Places to visit:

Hidden gems:

Recommendations for places to eat or drink:

Places to visit:

Hidden gems:

Recommendations for places to eat or drink:

Places to visit:

Hidden gems:

Recommendations for places to eat or drink:

Places to visit:

Hidden gems:

Recommendations for places to eat or drink:

Places to visit:

Hidden gems:

Recommendations for places to eat or drink:

Places to visit:

Hidden gems:

Recommendations for places to eat or drink:

Places to visit:

Hidden gems:

Recommendations for places to eat or drink:

Places to visit:

Hidden gems:

Recommendations for places to eat or drink:

Places to visit:

Hidden gems:

Recommendations for places to eat or drink:

Places to visit:

Hidden gems:

Recommendations for places to eat or drink:

Places to visit:

Hidden gems:

Recommendations for places to eat or drink:

Places to visit:

Hidden gems:

Recommendations for places to eat or drink:

Places to visit:

Hidden gems:

Recommendations for places to eat or drink:

Places to visit:

Hidden gems:

Recommendations for places to eat or drink:

Places to visit:

Hidden gems:

Recommendations for places to eat or drink:

Places to visit:

Hidden gems:

Recommendations for places to eat or drink:

Places to visit:

Hidden gems:

Recommendations for places to eat or drink:

Places to visit:

Hidden gems:

Recommendations for places to eat or drink:

Places to visit:

Hidden gems:

Recommendations for places to eat or drink:

Places to visit:

Hidden gems:

Recommendations for places to eat or drink:

Places to visit:

Hidden gems:

Recommendations for places to eat or drink:

Places to visit:

Hidden gems:

Recommendations for places to eat or drink:

Places to visit:

Hidden gems:

Recommendations for places to eat or drink:

Places to visit:

Hidden gems:

Recommendations for places to eat or drink:

Places to visit:

Hidden gems:

Recommendations for places to eat or drink:

Places to visit:

Hidden gems:

Recommendations for places to eat or drink:

Places to visit:

Hidden gems:

Recommendations for places to eat or drink:

Places to visit:

Hidden gems:

Recommendations for places to eat or drink:

Places to visit:

Hidden gems:

Recommendations for places to eat or drink:

Places to visit:

Hidden gems:

Recommendations for places to eat or drink:

Places to visit:

Hidden gems:

Recommendations for places to eat or drink:

Places to visit:

Hidden gems:

Recommendations for places to eat or drink:

Places to visit:

Hidden gems:

Recommendations for places to eat or drink:

Places to visit:

Hidden gems:

Recommendations for places to eat or drink:

www.ingramcontent.com/pod-product-compliance
Lightning Source LLC
Chambersburg PA
CBHW041605260326

41914CB00012B/1392